Santiago Calatrava: Conversations with Students

THE MIT LECTURES

Santiago Calatrava: Conversations with Students

THE MIT LECTURES

Cecilia Lewis Kausel and
Ann Pendleton-Jullian, editors

Department of Civil and Environmental Engineering
Department of Architecture
MASSACHUSETTS INSTITUTE OF TECHNOLOGY

PRINCETON ARCHITECTURAL PRESS

Published by
Princeton Architectural Press
37 East Seventh Street
New York, New York 10003

For a free catalog of books, call 1.800.722.6657.
Visit our web site at www.papress.com.

Material presented in this book is also available at
http://web.mit.edu/civenv/Calatrava/.

Printed and bound in the United States
05 04 03 02 5 4 3 2 1 First edition

Editor: Nancy Eklund Later
Designer: Deb Wood

Special thanks to: Nettie Aljian, Ann Alter, Nicola Bednarek, Janet Behning,
Megan Carey, Penny Chu, Jan Cigliano, Russell Fernandez, Jan Haux,
Clare Jacobson, Mark Lamster, Linda Lee, Jane Sheinman, Katharine Smalley,
Scott Tennent, and Jennifer Thompson of Princeton Architectural Press
—Kevin C. Lippert, publisher

Library of Congress Cataloging-in-Publication Data

Calatrava, Santiago, 1951–
Santiago Calatrava, conversations with students : the M.I.T. lectures
/ Cecilia Lewis Kausel and Ann Pendleton-Jullian, editors.
p. cm.
ISBN 1-56898-325-5 (alk. paper)
1. Calatrava, Santiago, 1951—Themes, motives. 2. Architectural
design. 3. Architecture—Technological innovations. I. Title: Santiago
Calatrava. II. Lewis Kausel, Cecilia. III. Pendleton-Jullian, Ann M. IV.
Title.
NA1313.C35 A35 2002
720'.92—dc21

2002003635

CONTENTS

PREFACE

IN NOVEMBER OF 1995, I was taking a sleepy walk in Valencia, Spain, when I saw this unusual but simple and very beautiful bridge. I inquired as to its architect, and the immediate response was "Santiago Calatrava, of course." I must admit that, at that point, I did not know who Santiago Calatrava was, but I am a quick learner and immediately proceeded to remedy my ignorance. At my request, a colleague, Professor Herbert Einstein, contacted Dr. Calatrava and began discussing ways to get him involved with MIT. It turns out that Santiago had already been invited to visit the school by the Department of Architecture. That visit gave us the opportunity to meet and to organize a series of lectures. This book, and its accompanying Internet site (http://web.mit.edu/civenv/Calatrava/), document the extraordinary exchange that occurred between Calatrava and a large audience of students and professionals over three days in 1997.

Hearing Santiago Calatrava speak reminded me of why I wanted to be a civil engineer. It reminded me of my own desire to create, to design solutions that are functional and beautiful, to leave behind works that will be remembered. I suspect that all civil engineers—and all children—have the same dream; unfortunately, our educational system conspires to dampen it. The idea of the architect-engineer has been lost. Creativity is buried under equations or hemmed in by the walls of specialties.

Calatrava represents what the architect-engineer should be. His bridges and public buildings reflect a

THE DIVORCE OF ARCHITECTURE and engineering is long standing and now, at least in the United States, almost ubiquitous. This divorce injures both parties. The ambition of architects to build well is diminished. Engineering becomes formulaic and uncomprehending of its social, environmental, and aesthetic dimensions.

As a school, MIT cannot exist independently from the conditions of our time and place, but we can foster ambitions to restore a profound alliance between architecture and engineering. Happily, there are those creative individuals who hold such ambitions and create exemplary works. In architecture, one thinks of Renzo Piano and his "building workshop," where building well is manifested even with the special challenges of building innovatively. But for all the excellence of Piano and his shop, he, like many other fine architects, works through a process of collaboration with the all-too-rare creative engineering firms. One thinks of Ove Arup in London, Buro Happold in Bath, and RFR in Paris, all of whom collaborate with architects to achieve works beyond the scope of either partner alone.

Especially in bridges, infrastructure, and long-span buildings, one finds engineers who control the entire design and succeed both in technical and aesthetic terms. Through our collaboration in the Felix Candela Lectures,* we have brought such practitioners to MIT, including Heinz Isler, Minoru Kawaguchi, Christian Menn, and Joerg Schlaich. Each of these engineers would be wholly convinced deep understanding of engineering. Like a classical arch, his structures seem to flow with the forces and, vice-versa, the force vectors seem to merge with the structures. There are no superfluous elements. The motion, real and apparent, of his creations is smooth and effortless, like motions in nature. Indeed, Calatrava commonly finds inspiration in the human body, the most beautiful and functional of all natural objects. His buildings, like the body, integrate individual elements through simple interactions to create enormously complicated machines.

Not everybody can be Santiago Calatrava. Not everybody is blessed with the same talent and artistic sensibility. Nevertheless, every civil engineer can strive to be more creative, and every architect, to be more imaginative and aware of the interplay between structure and mechanics. If we did, our professions would be far more exciting.

Rafael L. Bras

Bacardi and Stockholm Water Foundations Professor
Former Head, Department of Civil and Environmental Engineering
Massachusetts Institute of Technology

of the sound scientific principles their designs embody. Nonetheless we also observe a personal signature in their works.

Santiago Calatrava, architect and engineer, unabashedly pursues the unity of art and science. His exploration of natural forms (particularly of the human body), his readiness to work metaphorically, and his brilliance in representation all facilitate his creative exploration of form, space, light, and even kinetics. His mastery of engineering principles not only allows the realization of his designs but is challenged and advanced by the dialogue between formal invention and scientific principles.

The genius of this process is embodied in the energetic manner of Santiago Calatrava and powerfully advanced by the drawings that inform his lectures. We hope something of this dynamic survives in the static form of this book and will contribute to the larger ambition of promoting the fruitful common bond between architecture and engineering.

Stanford Anderson

Professor of History and Architecture
Head, Department of Architecture
Massachusetts Institute of Technology

*A series of annual Felix Candela Lectures was launched in 1996 by the Structural Engineers Association of New York, the Museum of Modern Art, and the departments of architecture of Princeton University and the Massachusetts Institute of Technology. Beyond honoring the creative achievements of Candela at the frontier of architecture and engineering, the series recognizes such excellence in current practitioners and seeks to advance these concerns through education.

INTRODUCTION

Ladies and gentlemen, I thank you very much for the opportunity to speak here in this school. After having been a student for a long time, studying in Valencia and then in Zurich for something like fourteen years, I started my practice as an architect and engineer. For sixteen years now, I have been working very intensely in this practice, and the only contact I have had with institutions like MIT is in sporadically giving talks. This is the first time that I have made a commitment to give a series of talks with the specific intention of communicating my experience. I think it makes sense now because these sixteen years form an important period in my life and because they define a generation—one stage in the life of a person. The things that I am saying I say for the next generation—the people who will look at my work and invent other styles and find their own way, just as I have integrated the work of those before me in finding mine.

I thought it best to speak about my own experience because, in fact, this is the only thing that I know. I mean to look back at the works that I have done and try to introduce you to the very essential thoughts that have informed my work during those years and the steps that have permitted me to go from one building to another, trying each time to implement a little bit more of my thinking.

MATERIALS AND CONSTRUCTION PROCESS

I choose to speak first about the idea of materials, because it seems to me that, in terms of architecture, materials are fundamental. After all, in architectural ruins you find only stones. So the material part of architecture—let's say the physical support of the architecture—is, in my opinion, very important and very fundamental.

I thought that a good first step toward understanding architecture was to understand what concrete is, what steel is, what wood is, how to use them, what they signify. What are the forms they can achieve? What are the differences between these forms? This is what I want to try to show you, beginning with the very first projects I undertook and continuing with the most recent works.

In this small figure done by using pieces of toys, the force of the hanging stone goes through all the pieces and is materialized in stone, wood, cord, and parts of steel. It seems very simple, but there is a lot of complexity there: the different pieces of the toy working in tension; the spindle that separates the parts working in tension, itself working in compression; even the colors that are put together in a simple but deliberate manner. There is no doubt that the simple act of holding a stone in the air can be a matter of expression.

The work that I did for the Wohlen High School in Aargau, Switzerland, required me to make a series of interventions in some existing buildings. I added an entrance, a central hall, a roof for the library, and another roof for the great hall. In this project, I changed materials several times. One part was built in concrete and steel; another part, in steel and glass; another one, in wood and concrete. Along with the experimentation with materials—using particular materials for particular solutions—I also introduced another theme. I thought that it would be interesting to work with the light, controlling it differently for each particular space.

The idea of the entrance was generated from the existing plan and its geometry. The plan was a trapezoid, which I cut with a diagonal to create a canopy that consists of two cones attached by an arch. One works in one direction and the other, in the other direction, with a pipe in cross section that provides torsional resistance and also holds the gutter. Even though the pipe has torsional stiffness, I used it here for the purpose of creating a link between the façade and the canopy, so that these elements work together in the same gesture. An ensemble has to become a single thing.

And of course, independent of the fact of construction, it is clear, looking especially at the elevation, that there is the idea of a leaf, or a palm. A very figurative idea was part of the design. There is certainly behind my very first approach—this free approach—to architecture a looking for inspiration in natural forms. The simple observation of things motivates me as much as the material aspects of architecture do.

The second intervention at Wohlen High School is an entry space. There I made a circular cupola in wood. The shape was very straightforward; a circle was subdivided into radial segments. These segments were made using a V that I cut, opening the interior. I replaced the portion of the crease that was removed with a linear element that signifies the compression in this element. I separated the different components of the cupola's support in order to make visible all the different types of support and to create a free ring around the periphery. This tension ring is floating. The idea of defying gravity is expressed in showing this ring—making it visible but not structurally significant—and then pushing back the corner supports of the V segments, which are the real supports of the cupola.

The light comes in from behind the cupola, at its base and through the creases of its triangular segments. The surfaces behind the cupola disappear in this light, so that you get the impression that the whole thing is floating in the interior space. It is clear, when you see all those shapes together, that they can be associated with petals.

In a library, the control of the light and the relationship of the light to the space is even more important. I thought it necessary to liberate the walls and to create tangential light, as Louis Kahn might do. I decided to make the roof at the center of the space seem to float. Its main support is a column toward which the roof inclines and through which rain water is channeled. The roof is a shell composed of several shells. The corners are held in place so that the roof will not move laterally, but all the weight is supported through the center column. Then light descends along the walls, tangentially.

For the genesis of the idea I started thinking about a book—an open book. Again, as in several other cases, the idea of the roof as floating came to mind. This is a theme in which the idea of lightness is embedded, and lightness is often created because of the contraposition of materials or of static systems. If the roof is heavy and the spindle is light, this contraposition of two materials combined with the light coming from the sides will make the whole roof seem to fly. The basis for the form of the shell was not the usual hyperboloid or paraboloid; it was a book—an open book. At the same time, the shell also wanted to become a bird. It is a kind of superposition of concepts. You can also see a leaf in it, held in the spindle support.

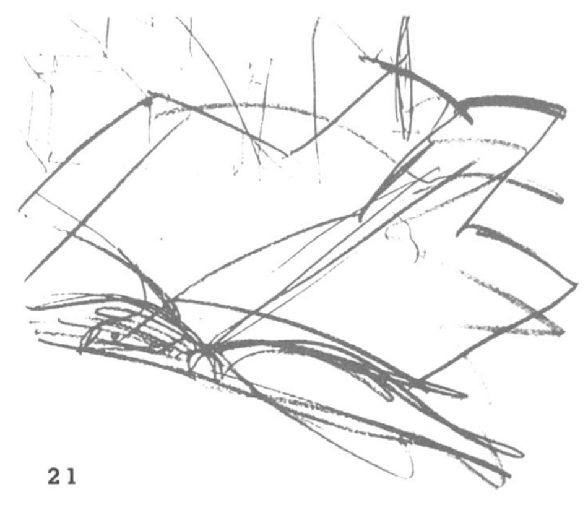

With the design of the great hall, or auditorium, what I wanted to achieve was quite simple. I proposed making the roof emerge by creating a parabolic arch on the interior that supports a raised shell that is independent of the walls. At each side of the shell is a gutter and a longitudinal window that brings light to the interior, very softly emphasizing the underside of the shell and bringing transparency to the repetitive, oblique elements that are transferring the weight of the roof to the arch. These oblique elements are all standardized pieces of wood approximately three inches by three inches. The parabolic arch and an upper arch supporting the shell are of laminated wood. The space is very intimate, partially because of the decision to use wood. The contrast between light and pattern on the interior also contributes to this intimacy.

As in the entrance canopy, there is the idea of a palm tree. Also—and this may be very figurative—I was trying to express the idea of the force of the parabolic arch transferring to the column. Many people think the column top is a reminiscence of an Ionic capital, which is not the case. It is more like the head of a ram.

The columns were pre-cast in concrete. I like very much brute concrete—concrete done on site—but pre-casting can be very interesting because of the complexity and freedom of forms that you can achieve. In Valencia, in my mother language, we used to say *formigó. Formigó* comes from *forma.* In Spanish, concrete is *hormigón* with "h" replacing the "f" of *formigó. Formigó* means material to which you can give form. This is a good definition of concrete. With pre-cast concrete you are very free to choose the shape, the texture, and many other characteristics of the material.

We cast the columns for the great hall in the most economical way. We cut the column in two and cast each half horizontally and then glued them together. This has another advantage in that all the exposed surfaces in the end are finished surfaces; you do not see any of the places in which you have been casting the concrete.

Ernsting's Warehouse in Coesfeld, Germany, is also an early work. It was an exercise in how to clad an existing warehouse and give it new signification. The first decision I needed to make was about the materials, which had to be very economical. So we decided to use concrete and crude aluminum—crude in the sense that it is the standard aluminum that you can get very easily. You can purchase it corrugated or flat—you can get it in many ways—and it is easy to work with.

We investigated how to transform this building, not only materially, but also thematically. The limitation of the material created a significant restriction; the idea of working with a theme—here, the "pintoresque"—allowed us a certain freedom. By "pintoresque" I mean like a painting; each façade should appear like a different painting executed in the same two materials. The material creates a unity, and the treatment of the material makes each façade different from the others.

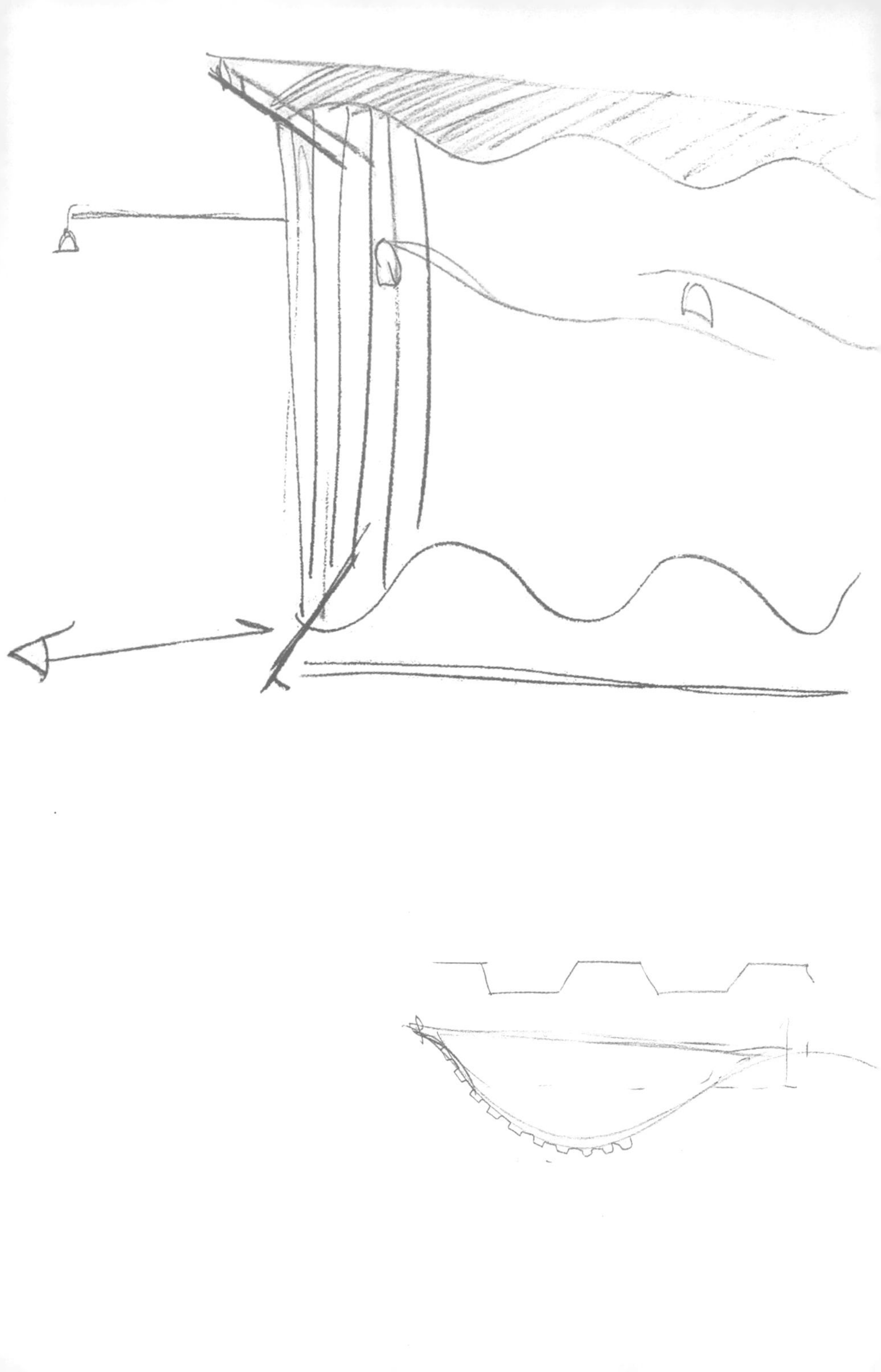

The south façade was done using corrugated aluminum, made into a sinusoidal curve. This gives the façade a double rigidity, because the convex segments of the curve are held at the inside with transversal connections. This curve gives one level of rigidity and the corrugation of the metal itself provides a second rigidity, permitting us to make quite a tall façade.

In order to emphasize the movement of the curve, we cut the façade at the top and bottom on an oblique angle, so that looking from the front, in elevation, the section of the sinusoid is even more accentuated. Looking up to the top of the façade, the curve is clear and readable. The client said that for safety reasons he needed a lot of light on the exterior, so we put lamps on the façade. The light makes the plasticity even more readable. We mounted the lamps away from the façade so that the shadows of the lamps follow the curve. They create drawings on the façade, and this is quite a plastic relationship.

This is the south façade, which means that the movement of the sun during the day makes a very significant change in the façade itself. In the curve you see shadows of the light and also the reflection of the sun. Vertical vibrations are produced by the reflection of the sun in the corrugations of the aluminum. The façade is extremely sensitive, changing with the hours of the day—with horizontal light, with vertical light. The oblique cut at the base makes the façade seem to float and move over the concrete structure.

On the north façade, the problem was different, because it has just zenith light—a very diffused light, ambient light. So how do you emphasize the plasticity of the façade in zenith light? I proposed using an S profile placed horizontally on the façade in very long pieces—as long as possible, which means maybe ten meters, or thirty feet, long. In this profile, the center section, on the diagonal, will generate quite a reflection. At the top edge where the two profiles overlap you will get shadow. Then again, less reflection at the bottom of the profile, until it breaks in shadow again. This makes a linear structure but one that is sensitized to the zenith light.

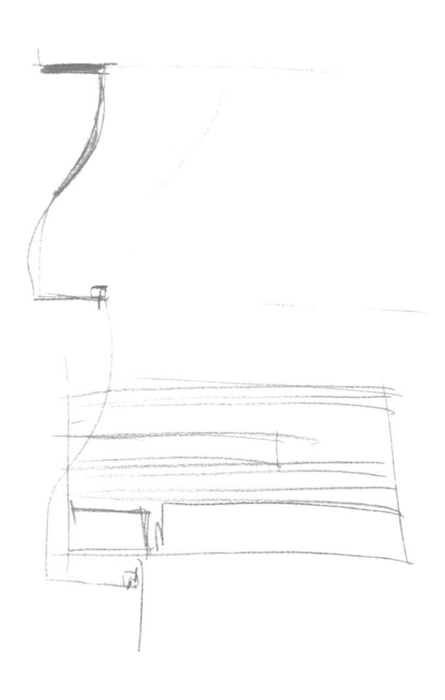

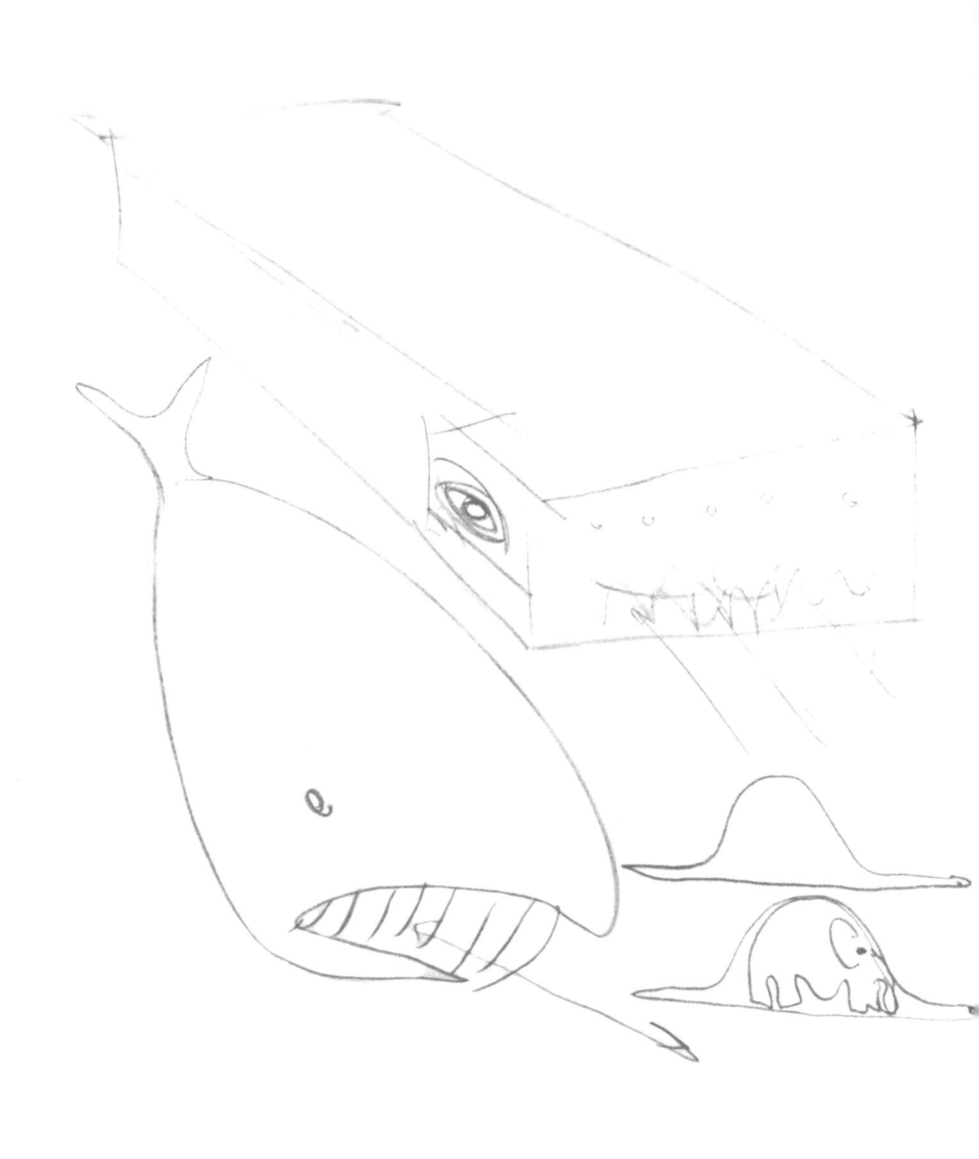

On the east façade we used corrugated plates seventeen meters high. The problem here was to put them on in one piece and to hold them in place with small elements at the bottom and the top. The east side is very flat, confronting the horizontal light of the morning sun. There was an elevator body on this side that needed to be clad. In order to distinguish it from the rest of the façade we used scales—like those of a fish—but very big ones, made of aluminum, that fold at the corners and into the top.

So again, each one of these façades is conceived as a separate picture. I spoke before of the "pintoresque," meaning like a painting. But how do you link these different paintings, these façades? From the very beginning, the building was like a foreign body. We had to find a way to give life to this body. The west façade has almost the same light conditions as the east façade, the sun setting versus the sun rising. It was also done using those very large panels of corrugated aluminum. It incorporates three large gates for the lorries that come in and go out every day. There are a lot of them. Many lorries wait at the door. The gates open and the lorries go in or out. If you look at these doors, at the building's scales, and at other things, the building somewhat resembles a whale. And with the lorries going in and out, it is like the story of Jonas, or like the elephant and the snake of St. Exupery. There is here a theme of swallowing. You see, it is also very important, this kind of game.

The sculpture I showed at the beginning of the lecture was made with toys. It was an exercise for me to take my children's toys and the things in my house—pencils, the cord that hangs the curtains, whatever I found—and make the sculpture. The elementality of the exercise, or of the thought, takes absolutely nothing away from the complexity of the solution. In the beginning something can be extremely spontaneous and simple. I want to walk. Where am I going? That is the question. But, you know, to walk is just a very natural thing, a very simple thing. A very long trip needs to be started with a small step. These thoughts of the whale are, in my opinion, an effort to pass from the "pintoresque" to the textual and to give the whole thing a life.

In the warehouse doors, the module is a continuation of the module of the façade. The pieces of the façade are all very repetitive; only the length of each has changed. In this there is a very beautiful idea. It is the idea that a façade can be transformed. The idea of transformation, of metamorphosis, is a mother of evolution in architecture—an unbelievable mother! It is not only because we can deploy mechanical and physical elements to create new architectures based on the idea of metamorphosis but also because we are maturing in our needs and in our understanding of culture that now is the moment to introduce these components into architecture in a major way.

Can you imagine, for example, a whole façade that gets transformed? Not just half a façade, like in this project, but the whole façade, like a curtain opening from one side to the other. This is, in my opinion, feasible today and certainly a challenge for the new generation and in the evolution of architecture.

The Stadelhofen Railroad Station in Zurich is sited on a hillside. In section, you have the lake of Zurich that used to extend to the base of this hill—a moraine made by glacial deposits. Early settlers walled off part of the lake to create a flat area upon which they started building. Later, the railroad came and made a cut into the hill for two rail lines. The cut separated two areas of very different character—a situation that is still preserved today; on one side it is very urban, and on the other side, very green.

Our exercise was to enlarge the station. It is a station that is heavily trafficked and one that is important within the regional railway scheme. Our intervention considered the fact that there was an existing cut from which we had to step back, cutting deeper into the hill. The basic idea was to conserve the original edge of the cut, so as to be able to retain the green condition above it. For this, we proposed a wall-like structure that is permanently anchored to the hill. The wall supports the houses built on it, which are often very close to the edge of the site. Gardens and a pergola were created along the wall, preserving the character of the upper part of the site and allowing for the possibility of people promenading above while passengers wait for the train below. Beneath the train lines we built an underground arcade for shops, which makes the link to the platforms more safe and more interesting.

There were many other issues technical in nature that conditioned the construction process. For instance, the site on which we worked was very narrow—sometimes only twenty seven meters, or ninety feet, in width. There were houses on both sides, so for technical reasons we had to go underground as much as fourteen meters, or about forty-five feet. Also, we had to build the project with the trains circulating the whole time; the traffic in the station was never interrupted, with a train arriving sometimes every two minutes. This was quite a challenge on such a tight site, especially in terms of staging and issues of safety.

I was very nervous because it was one of the first jobs in which I was responsible for the architecture and the engineering. This was a big thing, but I thought that we should also have some fun with the station. So in addition to relating the station to the functioning of the complex and to the urban context, I began for the first time to experiment with ideas of the body and of anatomy. I thought about gesture. I started with my hand and the idea of the open hand, which signifies sincerity and openness. From the open hand turned palm-side-down, I chose the area between the thumb and index finger as the shape of the column, which you then see repeated several times throughout the project.

I should also explain that the station is geodetic; it is not flat. The trains come out of a tunnel underground and go back into a tunnel. The two sides of the tunnel are curved downward in section, and only the center of the station is level. So we built the station slightly arched. The columns are inclined to remain perpendicular to the contour of the arch, but you don't see them as changing inclination one to the other. If they were vertical, you would immediately see it, but they are inclined in all directions. Even the underground gallery is like this. The station is also curved in plan. This was purely an engineering circumstance; the plan and section of the tracks were existing and had been done by engineers. But having a curve creates the possibility of making a station 280 meters long—approximately 900 feet—seem much longer than it is, because from the center platforms you do not see its ends. So the curves in both plan and section help the concept. You see, the shape, turning around like a torus, emphasizes the dynamics of the trains. Having this kind of rotational geometry makes it possible to achieve a dynamic effect in the architecture, especially through the repetition of elements.

It is interesting to observe that, in fact, the station is almost a non-station, because it disappears, hidden behind the roofs in the middle of the city.

I would like to make a small parenthesis to explain to you a different experience with concrete. I was charged by the Swiss Association of Concrete Makers to do a pavilion for an exhibit in Basel. For this project, I produced a machine that attempted to put concrete in movement. We know light concrete, we know heavy concrete, we know of all kinds of concrete, but concrete in motion is a rare thing. I don't know if you know Eugène Freyssinet, who was the inventor of the pre-stressing of micro-concrete to make wings for airplanes. This probably was never achieved, but he did all kinds of studies for this. This is to say that in the early twentieth century—in the '20s and '30s—people were extremely daring in their ideas and in their hopes for the use of this material.

In this pavilion I wanted to achieve forms that were extremely related to the body. By body, I mean the anatomy of the female and male bodies. I was interested in the idea of the sensuality of form. So you will see, maybe, ribs and circular elements that turn. It is a very tactile and soft way to use concrete that one does not usually consider. It is not only about moving the concrete but also about giving it sensual properties, like the properties of flesh or skin. The idea of "organicity" is even carried out in the details of how one piece joins to another. The shape of the detail becomes more than the result of an elaborate structural geometry; it permits us to recreate, as in a dream, the idea of the breast, for example.

The last project I would like to talk about is the Satolas Airport Railway Station in Lyon. You have to understand that this object was built by extremely careful and very gifted people using their hands to make the concrete. You have to understand the beauty of the construction site as a process, the way things are put together, the importance of getting close to the people working on the site, because they are fundamental. In fact, if someone risks their life it is certainly not the architect; it is the people on the site who do that.

The station is built in concrete, aluminum, steel, and glass, with granite paving. The concrete is white, using only white cement, natural aggregate that is taken from the area, and sand that is light gray. This gives a very light concrete, the color of which reminds you of the site. The roof is aluminum and reflects the sun. The façade of the train galleries is done using just pure concrete, with glass in between. The esplanade is made of granite cobblestones, and the handrails are all done in concrete. The large, open façades of the wing are in steel and glass. There are many different materials, but there are very precise rules for the way they are used. For example, the steel never touches the ground—it is always bordered by concrete. There is never a direct connection between a supporting element and the ground.

The wing of the station is oriented toward the south. We set the angle of the roof by the inclination of the sun on the solstice so that between the middle of June and November the sun does not enter the interior of the space. After November the façade lets light into the whole volume of the interior space. This permits us to have a building with very little need for extra climatization.

jo avido

certero, plácido, incisivo

instrumento físico orgánico

orden en consideración de [illegible]

sistema del arquitecto [illegible]

presión fuerte y la <u>puerta</u> de acceso

mundo de las ideas, cuya expansión

justa e inmediata y el gesto de

ojo y cabeza [illegible]

l exte [illegible]

ojo y a [illegible]

l interior [illegible]

Scultura

[illegible]

orden de la intuición, el orden del pensam

encuentran [illegible] otras imágenes juegan y cont

aquellas [illegible] percibida por el ojo

ideas

externo

I was interested in the idea of creating a structure that is based on certain proportions of the human body. Many of these bodies together support the train galleries of the station. The whole gallery is based on this modular.

The idea for the shape of the station and its roof was generated from the idea of the eye, and this is very important. Someone once said that if the painter Raphael had not had arms, he would have been a very good architect, because the working instrument of an architect is the eye. It is the faculty for seeing and judging and inventing things. There are two sets of eyes: the two eyes in front of us and the eyes of the mind that invent and combine things.

FORCE AND FORM

If we consider engineering an art—as I believe it is—and if we go back to a time when there was no difference between the art of architecture and the art of engineering, as I suggested we do at the beginning of my first talk, then we can consider that it is in ourselves, and especially in the new generation, that a rebirth of art happens. It is not only our heritage but also the mother of heritage that we must translate into action through our capacity to make buildings, reinventing them each time.

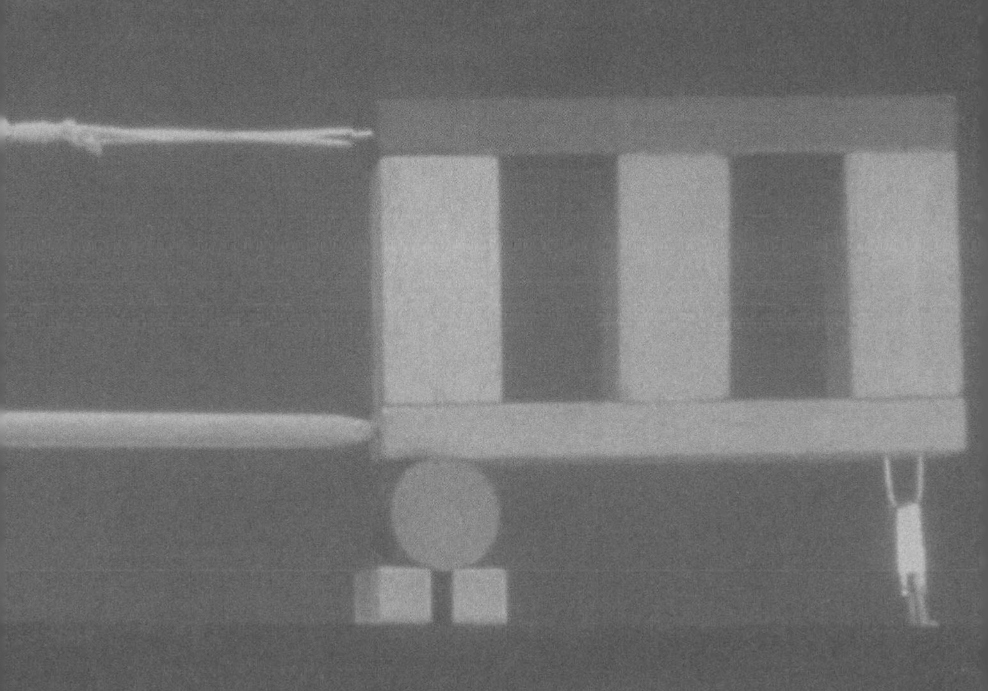

I would like to begin my second talk by showing another small object that is done using my children's toys. This one expresses another way of putting things together, hanging the same stone as in the previous case, but in this case, the forces are working parallel to each other; they do not cross. So it is like a game in which you discover that the weight of an object has the capacity to express something and that it all depends upon the ordering of the forces.

In my opinion, the consideration of the static properties of a bridge is very important. The bridge's static equilibrium is probably its most essential part, so that if we think of a bridge like a body, this static condition is analogous to the heart. Of course, the body has other parts; in a bridge you have other properties. The central part of the whole problem is certainly very much about resolving the problem of how to bring the forces from one shore to another.

One of the earliest bridges I designed was my diploma project done at the ETH in Zurich. The inspiration for this bridge comes from two different ideas. The first idea is of a cantilever bridge and the second is one of those beautiful arch bridges in which the forces are expressed by the arch. In a cantilever bridge, the forces work in another way. You have tension through the top and compression through the bottom, and then part of the bending moments are transferred into the shaft of the support. Beginning with the section of the cantilever bridge, I divided the material at the support so as to separate out these three forces, and I found that the idea of leaving a hole under the deck could be quite interesting.

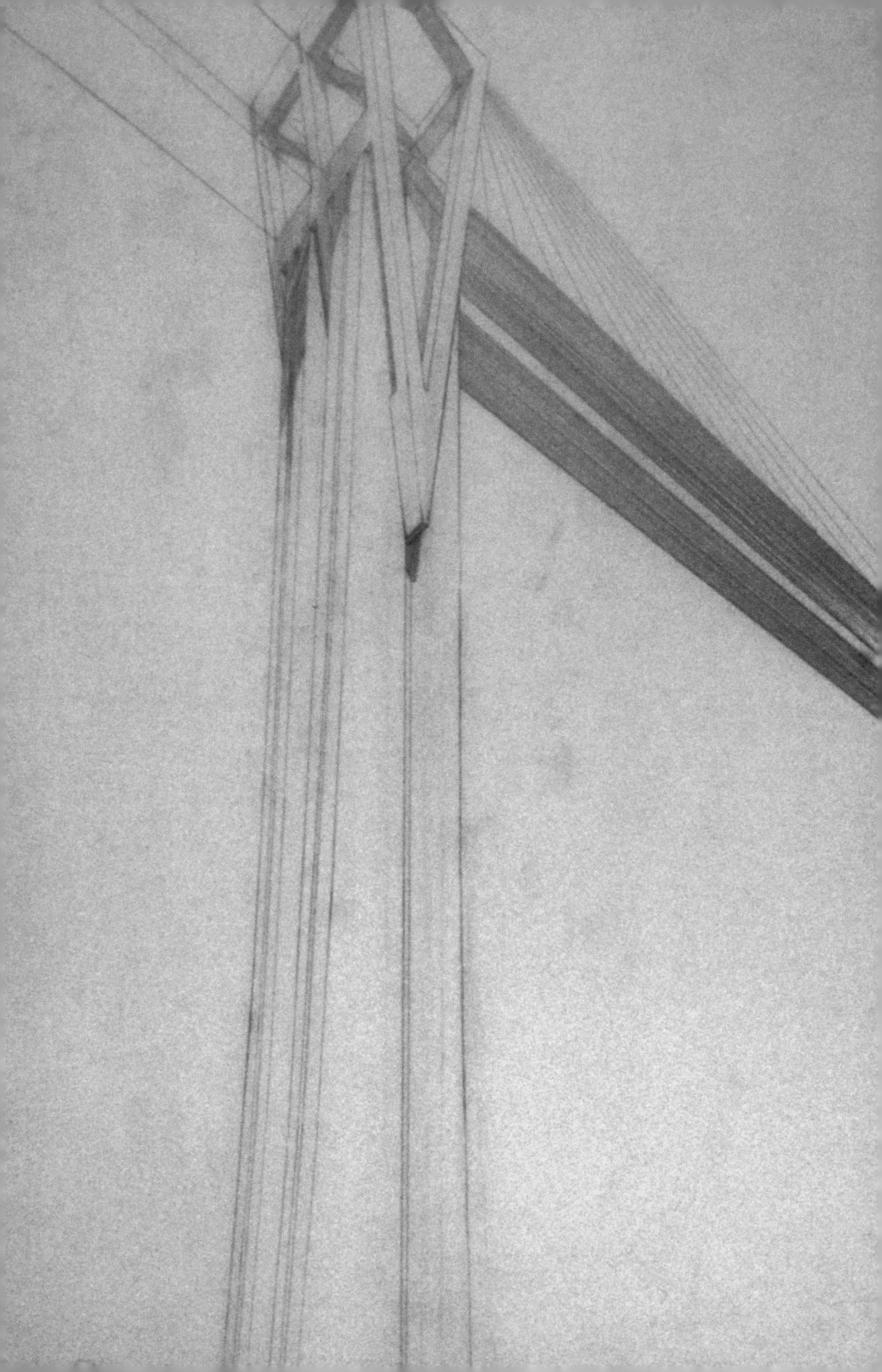

For the vertical support, I started with the idea of a pillar that has a certain proportion that today I relate to the human body. In fact, if you look at the pillar from the front it seems like the figure of a body with arms reaching up over his head to hold the deck. The lower support is located where this figure's head might be. Also, it is maybe a contradiction, but instead of making the bottom of the cantilever wider at the vertical support, I made it narrower to emphasize the independence between the upper deck, which needs to stay wide to conserve the dimension of the roadway, and the lower part of the cantilever, which is working in compression.

The first bridge I built and would like to talk about is the Alamillo Bridge in Seville. For the World Exhibition of 1992, my thought was to do two bridges that were symmetrical; one on one side of the island and another on the other side, with a viaduct linking them. First, I created the viaduct across the island—one that has many supports and is quite transparent. Then I generated the bridges in response to the scale of the space. These bridges were to have masts, which are the gestures that articulate this response.

For various reasons I could only build one of the two bridges. The design of the bridge was original; as far as I know, this kind of bridge had never been built before. Usually, in a cable-stayed bridge you have a compensation of the forces from the cables on the bridge side of the pylon to the cables on the anchored side of the pylon. However, if you incline the pylon, the forces are not only compensated for by the cables behind but also by the weight of the pylon itself. If the pylon is inclined enough and heavy enough, you can almost compensate the forces of the whole bridge purely through the pylon itself. This is what I tried to do here.

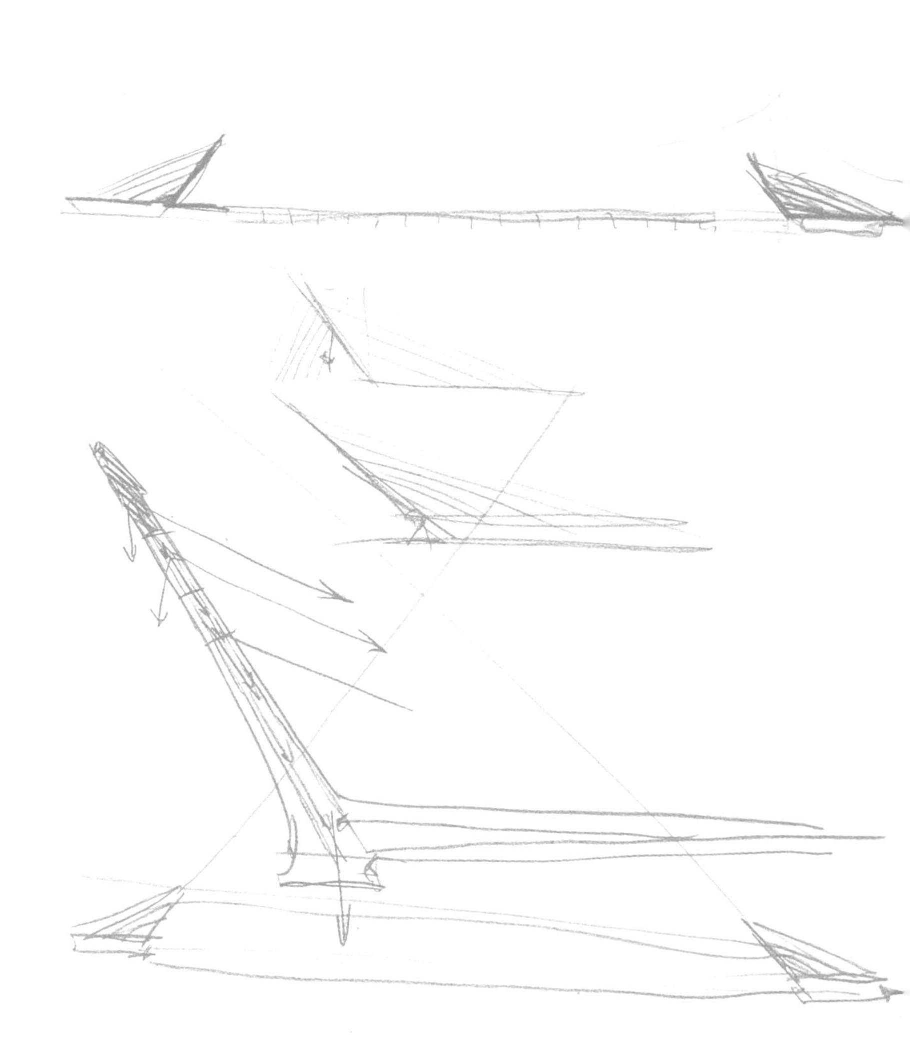

It is important to understand this object mechanically, and this will be one of the few times I will talk about this subject. You see, mechanically, what is happening is that each segment of the pylon or mast has a certain weight that pulls downward. Together with the tension in the cable, the resultant of these two coincides in direction with the mast. The next element of the pylon has then another weight—another force—and so on, and in each case the resultant stays in the pylon. Finally, the resultant compensates with the horizontal force coming from the deck and arrives as a pure vertical force into the foundation. The foundation is very small relative to the huge span of the bridge. It is interesting that, if the dead load produces a resultant at this point, then the live load will move it away. And then we have other problems, like the wind and many other things that we have to take into account in a cantilevering system.

Now I would like to return to my home town of Valencia and its river, the Turia. Valencia has a patrimony of bridges built in stone that, in my opinion, few other cities in this part of the world can claim; early Gothic, high Gothic, Renaissance bridges, all done using arches. These are magnificent works that we consider, without a doubt, as having architectural value. In fact, if you look at the old stone gates of the city and the Gothic bridge that leads to these gates, you see that there is very little difference between the architectural language of the gate towers and that of the bridge. There is another bridge that has not only huge public stairs but also chapels, and another—a concrete bridge from the early twentieth century—that has caryatids and other decoration executed by Terencio, a sculptor from the city. This is to say that if you go back a little, you come to a time when architecture and bridge building were absolutely linked together. The bridge builders were very conscious of this particular relationship. They were also conscious of the seriousness of the act of constructing a bridge. Many of those bridges are five hundred, six hundred years old and have resisted unbelievable floods. But even while taking into account the engineering needs of the bridge, the builders also thought about making small chapels (maybe to pray in, so that they would not be swept away in the next flood).

In this context I built a contemporary arch bridge over the Turia. It has a plaza below it and an underground station below the plaza. It is a pure steel bridge as much as the others were pure stone bridges. (I also built another bridge for Valencia, just outside of the city. Except for a few elements, the whole bridge is done in concrete.) In this one I divided the bridge's ramp into two, because first, it had to be very wide for traffic, and second, because it was the continuation of a boulevard that comes onto the bridge from one side. I chose to leave a void down the center of the bridge that corresponds to the space of the boulevard. In the space underneath the bridge, I wanted to emphasize the spatial effect. A pool of water is to be built in this lower space that will reflect light onto the underside of the bridge and also reflect the bridge itself. Light comes into this space from the sides and from above, between the pedestrian deck and the roadway.

Next is the Felipe II Bridge, built for the city of Barcelona. I would like to emphasize in particular with this bridge the capacity of a public work such as a bridge to generate infrastructure and in doing so, change the circumstances of a part of the city. The Bach de Roda area where this bridge was built was a very poor neighborhood—a kind of *bidonville*. The people who were living there were moved into better apartments so that the area immediately adjacent to the bridge and the train station below it could be turned into a series of parks. So, in a very rough part of Barcelona you now have a place that has the potential, in my opinion, to become a significant part of the city. In this case, the need to build a bridge and produce a link provided the impetus for regenerating a portion of the city.

One of the ideas of this bridge was to make a place. I made the bridge wider in the center, like a balcony, and the arches that span the railway tracks signify not only the bridge itself but also this place in the middle of this neighborhood. In this part of the city the landscape is not very romantic, but on the other hand, when I look at the mountains behind and the housing around, this space has huge potential to become a place of interest in Barcelona, especially now that there are green areas on both sides of the bridge.

I think that all cities need very much their public works to help them regenerate, especially now. During the '70s, architectural and urban interests focused on the historical point of view, which supported the regeneration of city centers to make them more habitable. Those interests also initiated the preservation of a lot of buildings that otherwise would have fallen victim to speculative development. But meanwhile, the development of the city's periphery began to become a very significant problem. So today, the problem is how to reform those parts of the city—and particularly European cities—where the population has doubled or tripled during the last thirty or forty years. I think that public works like bridges and stations can become very significant forces in regenerating areas by creating and focusing urban activity.

These next projects explore the idea of the arch. The first is a trade exhibition hall in Tenerife, in the Canary Islands. Sometimes when you design a functional building that, like many of the bridges, has to be done for a very low cost, the idea of using the arch is important. It is very efficient for large spans. In this building there are many different types of arches: concrete half-arches, and, on the top, steel arches. A large arch spans 240 meters—something like 800 feet—to support the whole roof.

COMSA

I would like to talk about the inclined arch in particular. The first example I will now show is the La Devesa Pedestrian Bridge in the city of Ripoll, which is in the northern part of Catalonia in the very dramatic landscape of the Spanish Pyranees. In this landscape we built a bridge to link the train station to a residential neighborhood located on the other side of the river Ter. The area between the bridge and the edge of the neighborhood was also transformed into a park, with a plaza and a series of interventions that were built by other architects. As I said earlier, bridges are very powerful when you want to regenerate a place, because they introduce a very good reason to restructure the surrounding area and, in so doing, make more livable these parts of the city that are rather lost, like this one here in Ripoll.

I would like to focus on the cross section of the bridge and the inclined arch, because there is a progression toward a rather bold asymmetry in the arched bridges as I have attempted to exploit the phenomenon of torsion. In the bridge in Ripoll, because the support—the arch—is offset to one side of the bridge, the weight of the bridge and its load create a torsional moment about the point of support. This torsional moment is put into a pipe section that runs the length of the bridge and connects the ribs of the deck to the inclined arch. In the bridge in Valencia, we transformed this pipe into the whole deck, so it is the deck that resists the torsion. In the case of Ondárroa, we have a lateral box girder and a cantilevering pedestrian walkway from which ribs spring to hold the arch against buckling, and from the arch we have tensional members that hold the lateral box. In the case of Orléans, the torsion is taken completely by the section of the roadway, which the arch supports just by cables.

So there is a kind of progression beginning with Mérida, where the arch is centered above the roadway deck, which is the element that provides torsional resistance. This is a large arch with three cords and is case number one. Case number two is Ripoll, which was for me a kind of experiment to control the system of the inclined arch in a span of 70 meters, or 230 feet, making it feasible at a very low cost and with a deck that is only something like 3 meters, or 10 feet wide. Case number three is Ondárroa, in which there is a significant traffic load, and case number four is Valencia, with four lanes of traffic. Orléans is case number five, with a major span, four lanes of traffic, and pedestrians on both sides.

What is interesting in this type of bridge is the torsion. In many of the standard cross sections that we see in arched bridges, the arch is straight up and so the torsional stiffness that we have in the box girder that supports the roadway is mostly unused, because you have only the unilateral load. What I have tried to explore in these bridges is the phenomenon of torsion—how to exploit the torsional resistance of the roadway to create a certain asymmetry in the bridge that permits me, for example, to emphasize the position of the bridge in relationship to the city around it, or the direction of the water, or even the position of the sun. It permits me to sensitize the bridge itself, as a phenomenon set into the surrounding landscape.

The landscape of Ondárroa is very picturesque with the Atlantic ocean in front, a small harbor, and fishing boats. For the Puerto Bridge, I tried to take advantage of local conditions and materials, using the stones of the area to build the embankments, for example. Many people walk across this bridge to Ondárroa's only beach, so it was necessary to provide an ample walkway. This brought me to the idea of making a big balcony on one side of the bridge. There is another pedestrian walkway on the other side of the bridge, but this one is given major importance by separating it from the roadway. With the hangers of the walkway, I made the bracing for the arch, which supports the bridge with cables. As with the bridge in Valencia, I was also interested in the space underneath the bridge. There are very large changes in the tides in Ondárroa and many people come with their boats to the area that surrounds the bridge. It was necessary to build big staircases going down into the water as part of the embankments. I separated the parts of the bridge so that the light can enter the space underneath, and this, together with the embankments, makes a very interesting space.

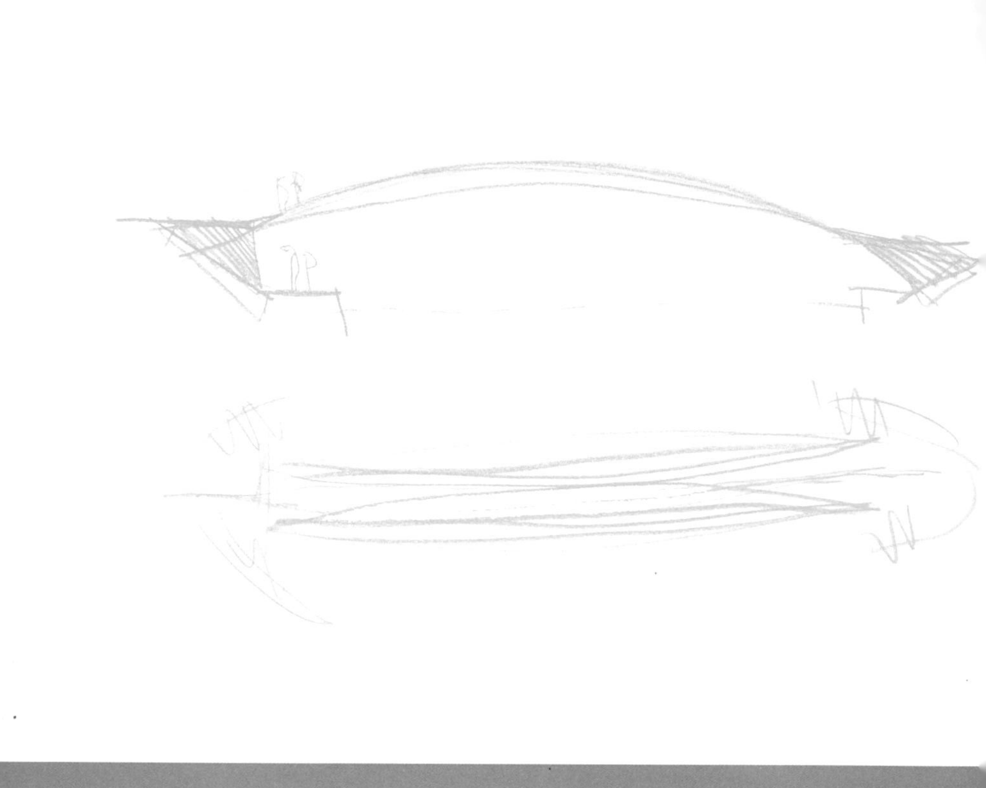

The Campo Volantín Bridge that I built in Bilbao is interesting because it is somewhat the antithesis of what I had learned—or thought—a classical bridge was, especially in terms of the embankments. If you think about a classical bridge, like the bridges in Venice, you have an arch and then all the forces of the arch are brought directly into the ground at the embankment, which is solid. This event is signified with a staircase, which permits the people to descend to the canal. The embankment is a classical element of the bridge; it is the way the bridge touches the ground as a continuation of the forces.

In Bilbao, I supported the bridge on cantilevered sections that rise up from the bank of the river and run parallel to it on both sides. The bridge deck is placed on these supports, which are like arms. The cantilevered section of the support is a half-arch, and so, where you usually would have had solid embankments, there are now voids. These voids and supports give a directionality to the bridge—one that can be associated with the direction of the flow of the river.

The flow of pedestrians runs parallel to the river, crosses the river, and then returns in the original direction. I signified this movement in a very simple way, by making a curve in the plan of the bridge. So the idea of the strict, straight line of a classical bridge disappeared as well. I wanted to make an element to hold this structure that—although asymmetrically placed—would optically compensate for the asymmetry of the deck. So the arch inclines over the deck counter to the curve.

The torsional pipe under the deck runs straight, so the particular point in which the arch and the torsional pipe come together is very important. Because the force of the arch is coming into this point diagonally—in section—and the force of the torsional pipe is coming in horizontally, the resultant of the forces displaces the vertical support necessary by several feet, revealing, in a way, one of the many paradoxical situations in the bridge: the support for the arch is three or four feet away from where it joins the torsional pipe, although it is centered in terms of the forces. I tried to play formally with a very pure understanding of the way forces of construction work in this bridge. For example, if you look at the plan of the bridge, you will see that the torsion is compensated globally, because the deck on one side of the torsional pipe is equal to the deck on the other side in surface area. At the end, we have the same torsional forces side to side.

Today we have somewhat lost the idealism of the '60s, when architecture was very much devoted to social problems. In fact, today we ignore these problems, yet we live in a world in which a third of the people do not get enough to eat every day. I mean, it is quite dramatic. Can you imagine how much infrastructure is still needed? If you think back to the heroic times of engineering, when people arrived at new places, imagine what it took just to bring water to a place, or to stop a flooding river, or to create sanitation infrastructure. I think you still feel the strength of this need when you build bridges, especially bridges in cities.

I also think that the potential of bridges and bridge design has not yet been achieved. The vitality of bridges comes both from necessity and from the fact that they are unbelievably significant, unignorable elements of the city. Could you imagine New York, for example, without those magnificent bridges? What if the George Washington Bridge was a multi-span bridge, instead of being this gesture jumping over 1,000 meters—more than half a mile—when the previous span had been just half that, or even less? Engineering can still provoke very wild and strong responses from gestures like these.

If you look at engineering design of the nineteenth century, you see that engineers took a lot of care in designing the handrails and the lighting. They were conscious that to take care of the details was to give more to the bridge. There are people that say "architecture is all that you can take away from a bridge to leave the bridge standing." This is not true. Architecture is the bridge itself, because the bridge is dedicated to man. All that gives satisfaction to man is good for a bridge.

MOVEMENT AND FORM

This evening I am faced with the task of giving you the third lecture, which is probably for me the most difficult one, because I would like to convey to you, in a way, the most intimate part of the work. This part is the cumulative result of ideas, sculptures, and drawings that have generated this or that building. In showing you these, I am acting somewhat like a cook who wants to give to other people—especially to young people—his secrets; what ingredients, what kind of herb or spices he has been mixing in to give this or that particular taste. Although the work is very personal in nature, it is also the culmination of many things that I have learned during my life...the approach of different artists...the approach of the idea of art...of the art of engineering...of the art of architecture, and of how these things can be linked together. So what I want to give you is quite a lot. For this reason, I will speak with very simple words, because that is the easiest way to communicate most directly.

In the first two lectures I began by showing small sculptures made from my children's blocks. The sculptures were not very big—something like one foot wide. In both, the problem was how to hold a stone hanging from these machines. If you look, it is only the change in the placement of the bearing (I want specifically to use this word, which is an engineering word) that creates two different ways of ordering the forces. In the first case, the forces are working parallel, and in the second case, they are crossing each other, but, in fact, it is exactly the same exercise—how to hold a stone. Relative to this, there are several things that I would like to emphasize. First, to hold a stone is, itself, something important, because you are working against the tendency of the stone to fall. Like the scientist who allegedly was hit on the head with the apple, we live in a field of forces and gravity that is immediate to us. Probably our bodies would be built completely different if gravity, or the forces around us, were other than they are.

Second, the sculptures hold together because the weight of the stone is activating the system. This means that, if the stone was not there, it would be very difficult to hold the machine together. So the weight, or the permanency of gravity, is also something that is materially present. The sculpture stays together because gravity is there and because gravity is a constant situation. What would happen if I were to cut the cord that transfers the weight of the stone through the whole system? It is very simple; the stone would fall down, and then, also, the small structure. When the stone falls down, a movement is produced. The forces of the machine are very much related, in their static condition, to this movement. This means that the presence of force is always related to a movement that cannot be established prior to its activation. Consider for a moment that forces are like crystallized movement. This is, in my opinion, quite a beautiful understanding, because even in its static condition, in the most stable thing, movement is hidden. A movement is there, and because of that I went from the idea of force and form, which I talked about in relation to my bridges in the previous lecture, to the idea of movement and form, which is much more difficult to represent in slides.

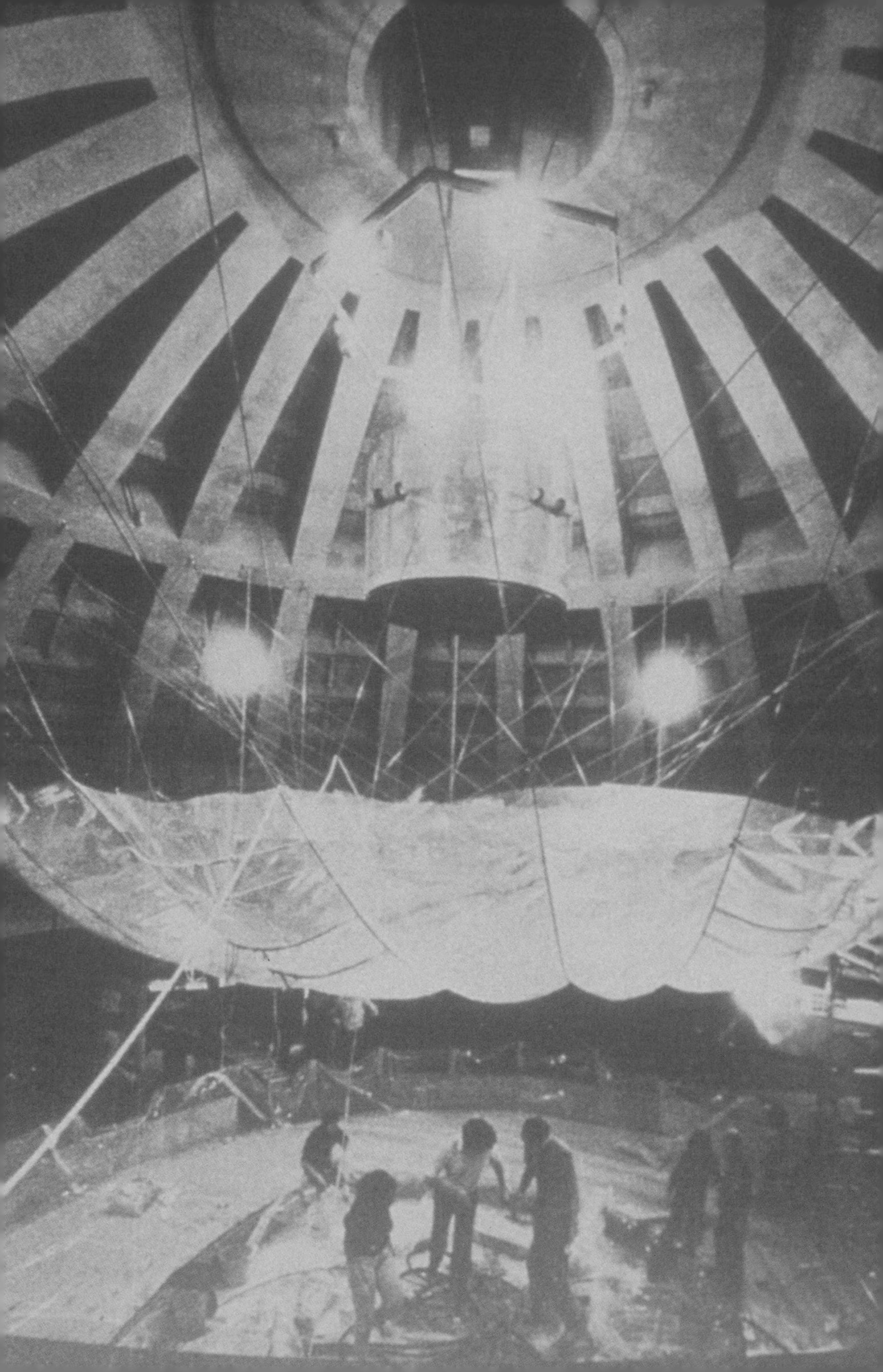

I would like to start by talking about two projects that were done while I was a student at the ETH in Zurich. The first project was done with a group of students under the direction of Jürg Altherr. We built a swimming pool hanging from the cupola of the ETH. It was hung by twenty-four wires that supported twenty-four ribs and a skin of polycarbonate that was 1.2 millimeters thick. It contained twenty-four cubic meters of water, and it was even possible to swim in it, although it was not possible to remain in the water for long because the pressure of one's feet might have broken or deformed the membrane. The construction was a very particular challenge, because below the cupola, under this swimming pool, was the library. Can you imagine? All that water over the library?

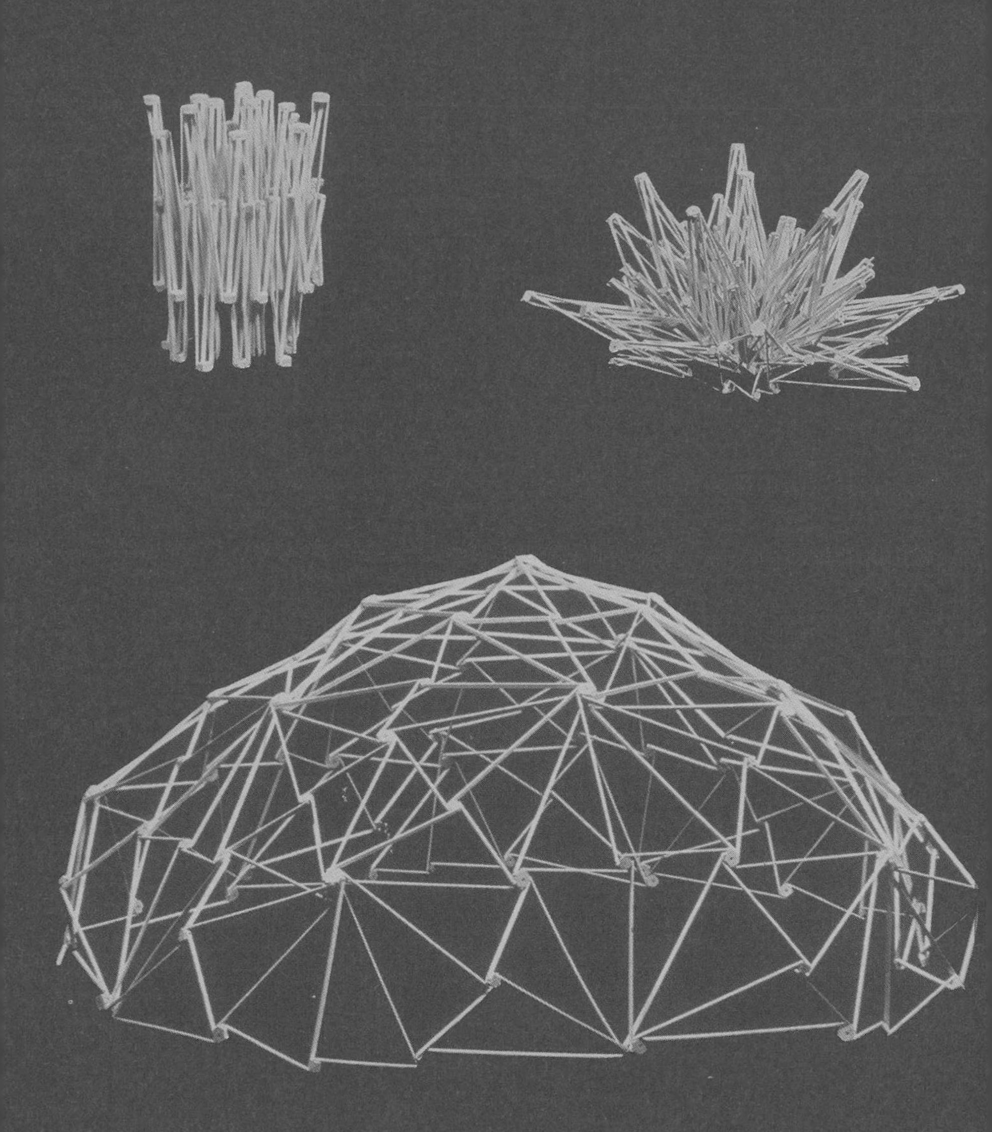

Different from, but not unrelated to, this idea of holding something heavy, the second project was a study of the explicit movement of polyhedra. My doctoral thesis was called "On the Foldability of Frames," and its basic focus was on the study of topology and the way in which a polyhedron—a very complex polyhedron—could be folded or transformed to become a bundle in which all the lines are parallel. Through a series of phases, this bundle opens, slowly changing its shape to recuperate the major polyhedron, which approximates a dome. Even if it did not look extremely good, the focus was on the complex geometrical process of changing shape from bundle to half-sphere.

Another source of interest that I would like to emphasize is nature and the very simple observation of nature, meaning to look in a straightforward and pure way at the natural objects that are around us: trees, grass, flowers, or whatever the natural object. From a group of study sketches, one early model that I made attempted to take the structure of a tree and apply it to an idea for a group of trees using steel and glass. I was no longer thinking in terms of the specific qualities of the object itself, but rather, through a kind of systematic approach to the object, I decided to make them transformable, meaning in this case that they change their form. So the ribs at the tops of the trees—configured as the roof—hinge at the point at which they are supported, and the entire roof opens through a mechanical transformation. The idea of the trees was later incorporated into a project for a gallery in Toronto. The idea of mechanical transformability, however, was not incorporated into the trees but into a very large, operable window that separates the gallery, which is quiet, from Heritage Square, which is a noisy, animated space.

Continuing with the idea of the tree—an idea that is quite general, in my opinion—we built the Orient Railway Station in Lisbon. Here, I used the same vocabulary, specifically choosing it because the city of Lisbon is not only very beautiful, but also has the very, very soft character of cities on the Atlantic coast. The space is very transparent, with a beautiful quality of light. In this context, I did not want to do a very strong structure, like in Lyon, but a soft one—an open structure with the trains passing on one side and the view passing on the other side.

Another topic that is also very important in architecture is anatomy and the idea of reading in the human body structures, or appreciating in the human body a sense of architecture. Whatever we do, the magnitude or the dimension of a thing is always related to our bodies. Architecture, in a very natural way, is purely related to humans, because it is done for—and by—people. This makes anatomy a very powerful source of inspiration. And this was true not just in the Renaissance, when the human anatomy was the basis for rules and proportional systems, but also in the twentieth century with the Modulor. Anatomy—the idea of the hand, of the open hand, the idea of the eye, the mouth, the skeleton—is a rich source of ideas and inspiration. In the tectonics of our own bodies, you can discover an internal logic that can be valuable in the making of buildings.

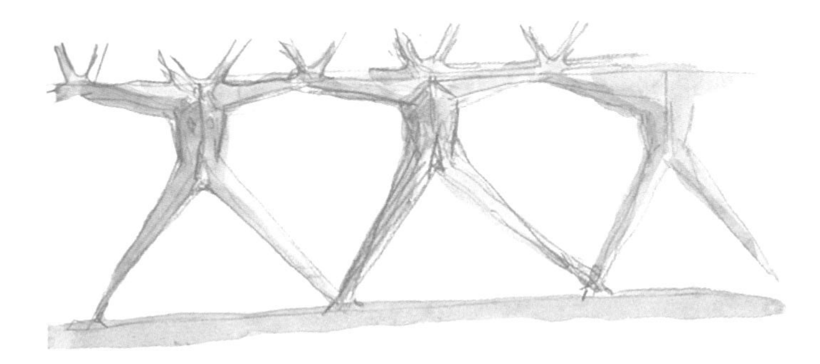

It is important to recognize in the phenomenon of architecture its purely plastic or sculptural aspect. This is not in conflict with the functional aspects of architecture, nor with the structural aspects. The wings of the station in Lyon, for example, take their geometry from a sculpture that was done previously as a study on the eye.

More abstract than my studies on the eye are my studies on how the head is supported in a position over the shoulders. Why and how can I turn my head? The entire mass is supported only by the atlas of the vertebral column, and so the head can move. This wonder of moving the head—rotating it, inclining it, or both simultaneously—is quite interesting and, in a way, quite dramatic. I have been studying how to hold the head. I begin with a pure volume and mass—a cube—trying to hold it with a minimum amount of elements; for example, with a very, very thin spindle and a series of cables around it. In another sculpture, the mass, or head, is supported vertically by one element and a second oblique element is used to push it back—to fix it in its horizontal position. In the section of the Stadelhofen Station, the same principle is used, but the mass that is represented is a cube and the sculpture is the earth.

I like very much the purity of a single idea, just as the pure expression of a single note can be a very powerful thing. Complexity comes from the superposition of ideas in a coherent way. This means that, although each one of those ideas is capable of living independently, you can also put them one over the other, like a painter who works not only with black but with several colors, or hides a lot of blue behind the painting in order to capture the horizon. So, for example, in Stadelhofen, in addition to the reference to the

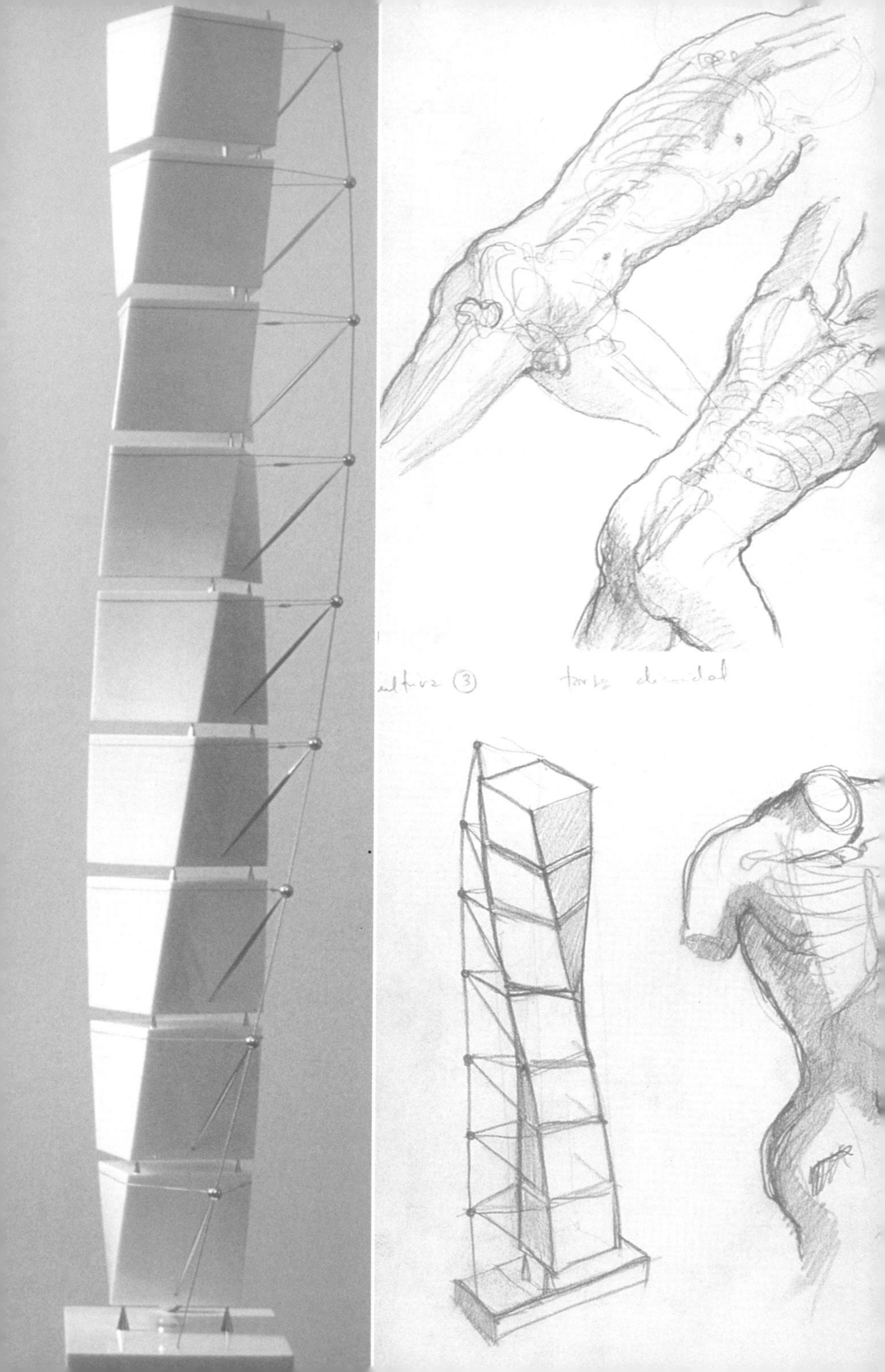

propped head, there is also the idea of the hand—the open hand. This reference is represented throughout the project. It became a leitmotif for the configuration of most of the structural members of the station: the main buttress supports, a small canopy, the pergola. The hand mirrored makes the cross section of the underground. In many places there is a gesture that can be associated with this same geometry.

Another important series of plastic studies goes a step further. They describe the spine, or how our body stands up. The spine is made up of vertebrae that are represented in the sculptures in a very elemental way, as a series of cubes.

Once you have the concept of the spine, it is very easy to move the elements around, reshaping the spine in several ways. In one case I staggered the position of the cubes around the central cord. In another they are stepped out so that the idea of movement is much more explicit. Although the material is the same, the hieratic rigidity has disappeared, so that you now have more the idea of a curving spine. Also quite important is how our spine twists, how it turns around an axis, and how it bends and reaches. What before was quite a shy movement becomes very explicit.

In some later studies, I changed the geometry of the cube in order to make the sculptures bigger. In one project that is twelve meters, or forty feet, high, I wanted to create a more organic shape, and so I moved away from the cube, using double pyramids, or octahedrons, instead. There is a series of seven of these octahedrons in concrete, one after the other, each held back by two pins and a single cable. The seven pieces are counterbalanced by two very long legs. At this scale, the sculpture is now more than an abstract form; it is also a construction principle. This sculpture became the basis for the bridge I built in Seville.

Starting with a very pure and abstract study of the human body and anatomical relationships of weight, one can move through to a major problem in steel. When you start building a sculpture that is twelve meters high, the construction problem begins there. How to hold things, how to choose the material; these issues become critical. You have to deal with concrete. You have to deal with cables. You have to deal with supports and with tensions, with transport, and with many other things.

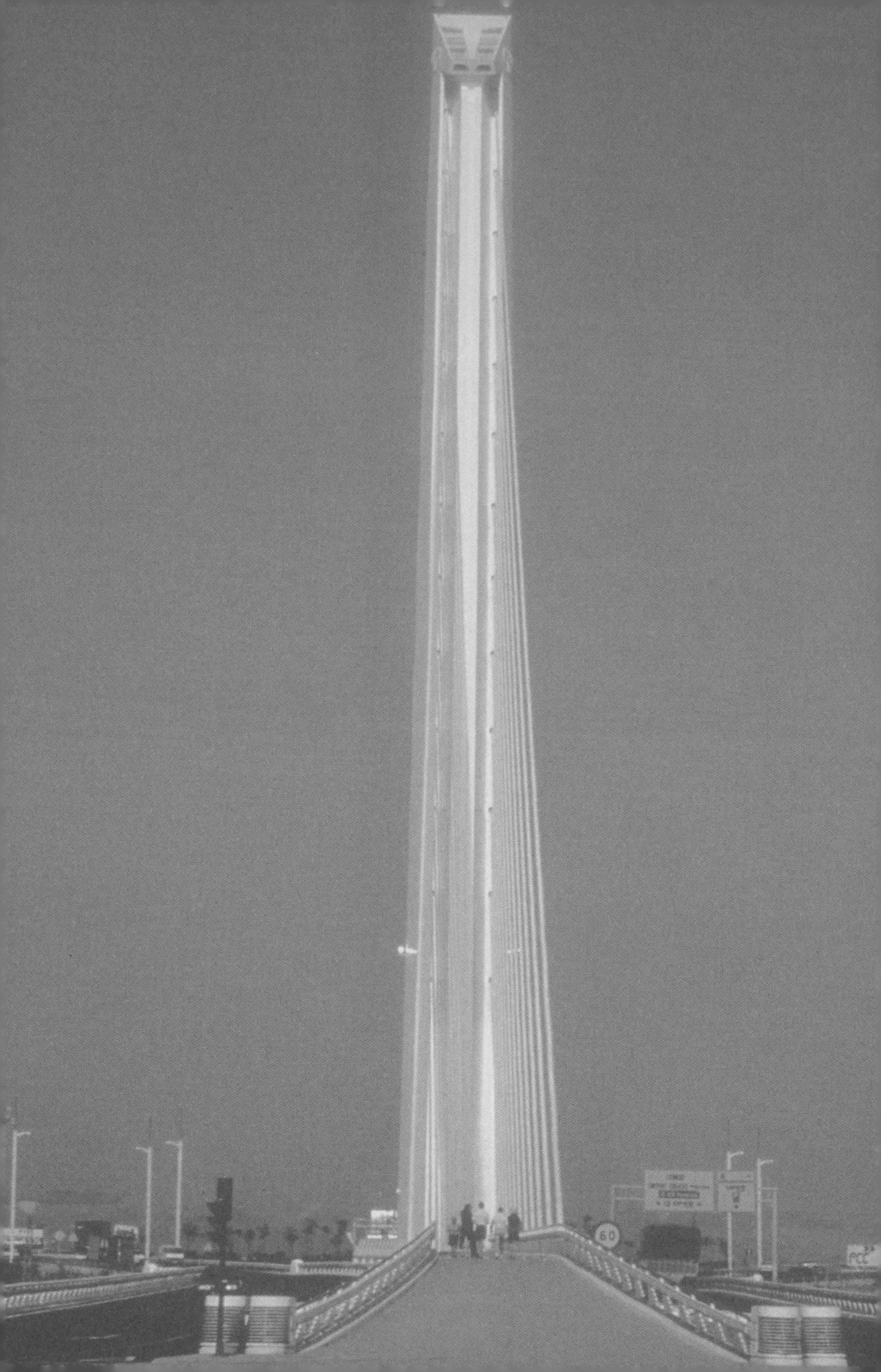
60

In particular views of the bridge in Seville, you can recognize the very abstract origin of the bridge's idea. When you look at the bridge from the front or from the back, you do not think of a bridge. Instead, it is the expression of something autonomous. A plastic or sculptural exercise is very beautiful in itself, because you feel free. You are only bound in terms of the limits you set, saying, for example, "I would like to be extremely orthodox. I will work only with cubes." Whatever the specific terms, you have limited your vocabulary, but you are still free, because the only goal that you are pursuing is a pure plastic achievement. When you are dealing with a bridge or a building, even if it is a plastic event, you are bound by functional needs. On the other hand, you have a big advantage, which is scale. No sculpture in itself will ever reach the scale of a bridge or a building. It is this that gives architecture— and particularly, architecture that is integrated with engineering—its significance.

Here I would like to talk about some research that is related to movement, but more specifically, to simple structures that can move. We built a pavilion for the State of Kuwait at the World's Fair in Seville, and it is done using a series of wooden half-arches that can open. This structure covers a terrace, the floor of which is made of translucent marble. Below this terrace is the interior part of the pavilion, and during the day sunlight is filtered through the marble to light up the interior space. The roof elements are supported by concrete members, and each one of them can be activated by an individual motor so that very slowly the whole roof opens and transforms. Because the elements are independent, you can control the different stages of the roof's opening. In the movement of the roof, one can imagine the hands with their fingers bent down, serving to protect the space, and then opening, palms up, to cup the sky.

A sculpture that we did for the courtyard of the Museum of Modern Art in New York was placed beside a weeping willow. The branches of the willow are gently curved. The branches of the sculpture are also curved, and they fall slowly—each one turned by a wheel—to almost touch the sculpture of *The River* by Aristide Maillol, which is below, on the surface of a pool.

From a series of sculptural studies that were based on the idea of movement—and specifically, the idea of topological surfaces that are generated by straight lines that revolve around multiple centers—came another set of studies for a possible roof structure. In these sculptures, straight lines generate folded, curving surfaces. In subsequent architectural studies, these straight lines became single elements of construction. You have a shape on the ground, then one central inclined ridge line, and the identical construction elements connect the profile of the shape—which is a circle in one case and a half-ellipse in another—to the inclined line. This same study was also a source for ideas about how to make this type of form move and open. The two halves connected by the central line are like two hands that are hinged together at the thumbs. They open up and close down around the axis of this hinge.

The extension for the Milwaukee Art Museum, which we are now building, uses a variation of this roof structure. In my project, I linked the original building by Eero Saarinen and the extension by David Kahler, built something like twenty years ago, back to the city with a bridge. This existing museum is, itself, like a bridge, and, in my opinion, what I have done is very respectful of the idea of this museum and its relationship to the city. In the existing museum you have a bridge and a sculpture-like volume in front of the lake; in my project you also have a bridge and another volume in front of the lake. While the existing volume is compact and closed, this new volume is transparent. A very shallow shed building links the new extension to the old extension, permitting from the height of the bridge a view of the lake's horizon beyond.

So as to conclude with architecture, I will speak about the cathedral of Saint John the Divine, which was never completed. It was started by Heins & Lafarge and continued by Ralph Adams Cram, with some work done on the vaults by Rafael Guastavino. Only the nave and apses exist today. In a competition entry for the cathedral, I tried to implement some of the vocabulary you have seen before but in a more symbolic way, because symbolic language in a cathedral is very manifest. I thought of comparing the cathedral to a tree, with the roots at the bottom, the trunk, and then the foliage at the top. One task of the competition was to create what they called a "bio-shelter." The bio-shelter was supposed to be on the interior of the cathedral, but I thought it better to put it above. The vaulted space in between the cathedral's interior space and the roof is usually dark and closed. I wanted to open it up.

The idea I proposed was to replace the roof, which is temporary today, with a glazed roof and to plant trees in this upper space so as to create a garden over the cathedral. The garden would be a reproduction of the temple itself. It is interesting that in the work of Beethoven—for example, in the fantasy for choir, orchestra, and piano—they sing about *Im Tempel der Natur*. Nature is considered a temple. And so we were thinking about making this temple of nature. This is a very romantic idea.

The plan of the cathedral follows a Latin cross. One can look at the human body as a temple, and inside the shape of the Latin cross can be found the idea of the human body. So the garden and the body are superimposed and related to the geometry of the cross. This kind of mysticism that comes from a far away time was part of the conception of the building.

I wanted to make the glass roof of the garden operable, so as to let the rain water collect in the garden. The triangular sections of the glass roof function in a way that is similar to the big windows in the gallery in Toronto. They just turn around an axis. The roof was designed with a very high spire, which could be used for thermal purposes, to create a microclimate on the interior of the roof.

To approach the natural world with respect, to approach the landscape with much more respect; this is a concern of architects and engineers. And I would like very much to underline this, without going too far into this theme, but the integration of buildings into the landscape is something very important. I think that in the basic idea that we submitted for Saint John the Divine there was an interesting equilibrium.

CONCLUSION

All these projects in which I have been working have been possible not only because of the people who have executed them—and who I appreciate very much—but also because many people have been helping with their hands and their eyes. Making models, making drawings, in my office. They have all participated in this effort and have contributed a lot to the projects. My wife has helped me very much in these talks. Thank you very much to everybody.

This defines the end of my talk. I would like to thank you very much for your attention.

SANTIAGO CALATRAVA VALLS is one of the most important figures working at the intersection of architecture and engineering today. Born in Spain, he maintains practices in Zurich and Paris. His innovative and undisputedly expressive bridges, train stations, airport terminals, concert halls, and art museums—and the remarkable sketches he creates while designing them—have been the subject of numerous books, including *Calatrava, Public Buildings* and the two-volume *Santiago Calatrava's Creative Process*, both published by Birkhäuser.

CECILIA LEWIS KAUSEL is professor and director of the Interior Design Department at the Chamberlayne School of Design at Mount Ida College in Newton, Massachusetts. She received BA degrees in biology and physical anthropology from UMASS and an SM from the Department of Architecture at MIT. A guest professor at the Bauhaus and a research affiliate at MIT's Department of Civil and Environmental Engineering, Lewis Kausel has published numerous journal articles and a report on the preservation of the Alhambra for CEDEX, in Madrid.

ANN PENDLETON-JULLIAN is an architect and associate professor at MIT. After studying astrophysics for three years, she received her BArch from Cornell University and her MArch. from Princeton University. She is the author of the award-winning book *The Road That Is Not a Road and the Open City, Ritoque, Chile* and several other theoretical works. Her architectural work has been published and exhibited internationally.